Conversations

Listening In as
Real Guys
Pick Up
Real Girls
in the Real World

Nick McLaren

Copyright © 2002, Nick McLaren

All rights reserved. No part of this book may be used or reproduced in any manner whatsoever without the prior written permission of the author, except by a reviewer, who may quote brief passages in a review.

ISBN 0-9709719-1-5

Printed in the United States of America

Contents

Introduction   7

Hugging the Bar	11
Trying Too Hard	14
Conversation Primer	19
Opportunity Knocks	28
With Friends Like This…	30
He Who Hesitates Is Lost	33
Spontaneous Combustion	36
Guts but No Glory	39
Down on Me	42
The Anywhere Man	45
An Attractive Offer	48
Mother Knows Best	51
What a Joke	54
Missed Signals	57
Staying Focused	60
Open to a Fault	64
Go for the Gold	67
And a Little Embarrassment for Flavor	72
Antidepressant	76
Slow Motion	81
Battle of the Sexes	86
Figure This One Out	91
No Go	95

Conclusion   98

Introduction

There is no single correct way for a guy to approach and impress a girl. In fact, there are as many ways to meet girls as there are guys and girls. Actually, there are more, because no one guy is going to use the exact same approach every time he runs into the opposite sex. On the other hand, while there are innumerable varieties of approach, there are also certain rules that you violate at your own risk. This book is designed to mold your behavior and conversational skills so that these rules of success with women work for you and never against you.

Having bought this book, you may already have read its companion book, the ultimate authority on meeting women—*50 Secrets of Picking Up Girls*. If you haven't, you should, because *Conversations* illustrates and expands on the concepts described in *50 Secrets*, giving you detailed examples of how these methods are applied "in the field."

What follows is a series of actual conversations between real guys and girls who have just met. Some of the guys do well, while others demonstrate that they have lots of room for improvement. As you read about these encounters, keep in mind that you can learn as much from a guy who blows it as you can from a guy who does everything right. Guys who do everything right are pretty rare. You're far more likely to recognize yourself in the ones who are rough around the edges.

This book will put you far ahead of the average guy, but it is only a book. I can't go with you on a Saturday night and point out all your individual strengths and weaknesses in handling women. What this book (and *50 Secrets of Picking Up Girls*) will do is give you the raw materials of success, show you where you need improvement, and more importantly, provide you with the tools you need to analyze, understand, and correct your own methods.

More often than not, guys make the same mistakes over and over—and never realize it. A girl you've just met won't tell you where you've gone wrong. It's not reasonable to expect her to give a total stranger constructive criticism— "Hey, Mr. Cool, if you made some eye contact now and then, you might do better with us women."

Nor is it likely that your friends will help you out. Chances are they know even less about women than you do, and besides, even if they are your friends, they are also your competitors. Your buddies may decide that there's little advantage for them in showing you how to be more effective with the girls they're also trying to win.

One of the most valuable insights I can offer you in this book is the ability to do self-analysis. You need to be more aware of how women perceive you, and you need to be able to look at yourself honestly in order to recognize and perfect your own methods.

To heighten your ability to do self-analysis, I will give

you real life conversations between guys and girls who are meeting for the first time. Then we will carefully examine what happened, what the mistakes were, what the great moves were, when the guy won or lost the girl, etc. It will be an experience similar to that of a football coach reviewing a game on videotape with a player, pointing out how the player could have taken advantage of all his opportunities. Like a coach, I will show you how to find the areas that need work in order to increase your performance.

You are probably wondering how we were able to capture these conversations. It wasn't easy. For the most part, we had to play James Bond in order to create this book. Whenever possible, we tried to record conversations in which neither the guy nor the girl knew that we were eavesdropping. In most cases, we used a variety of small recording devices purchased at a local "spy shop." In others, we actually hired a secretary skilled in shorthand, gave her a pen and note pad, and then had her unobtrusively take down conversations that we couldn't get with a recorder.

The primary objective of this secretive recording was to avoid influencing or intruding on the natural course of these conversations. We wanted to get recordings that were as real and spontaneous as possible.

The names of all our subjects have been changed (or made up if we didn't know the names) to protect the innocent and the not so innocent. In addition, most of the conversations were cleaned up grammatically in order to make them easier to read. An exact reporting of dialogue would be difficult to understand because people usually speak in a choppy manner, using expression, body language, and tone to fill in meaning. We've also deleted most of the "uhs" and "ahs" that people mix liberally into their speech, especially when they're male and meeting beautiful girls for the first time. (Hint: We all use "uhs" and "ahs" in conversation to give ourselves time to think, but frankly if you use them too often, they make you sound hesitant and less than brilliant. Make an effort to keep them to a minimum.)

Well, that's about all the introduction you need. Now let's get down to business.

Hugging the Bar

Our first conversation occurred in a large and popular nightclub. Two guys are leaning up against the bar, beers in hand, surveying the women around them and on the dance floor.

Bill: This place is packed!

Ron: It's always like this on Thursdays. The women come all the way from the Valley to be here tonight.

Bill: And we're going to make sure they don't go home disappointed, right dude?

Ron: We're here to please. Hey, check out the girl over there with that tall guy.

Bill: Damn, she's perfect! Perfect!

Ron: But taken.

Bill: Yeah, taken. Please God, let me do as well as him tonight.

Ron: Bill, what do you think of those two blondes over there? You want to go talk to them?

Bill: Maybe, I don't know, they aren't that good lookin'.

Ron: They aren't that bad lookin' either.

Bill: Let's finish our drinks and reload. Then we'll go over and check 'em out.

Ron: Bill! Those are some pretty awesome women. Come on, let's go over there before someone else grabs them.

Bill: Relax, Ron, we just got here. Have another beer, loosen up, then we'll talk to them.

Ron: Too late, they're talking to some guys now.

Bill: So what! There's plenty of women hotter than them. Man, there are some ladies here tonight with unbelievable bodies! You want another beer or not?

What's wrong with this picture? These two are going to be hugging the bar all night, watching, judging, speculating, bragging, but never actually speaking to a female. At 2:00 a.m., they'll leave and spend the trip home wondering why they never seem to get lucky.

Of the two, Ron seems to be more aggressive, but he allows Bill to hold him back, so he's not that daring. If Ron had been smart, he would have told Bill to hold his spot and then marched straight over and introduced himself to the two blonds. The other problem is Bill's I-won't-budge-unless-she-looks-like-Cindy-Crawford attitude. Of course, even if a girl did look like Cindy, this guy would be too intimidated to move a muscle.

Let's face it, Ron and Bill are paralyzed by the fear of being rejected. They're waiting for some kind of mythical sure thing that won't involve any risk. Unfortunately, there is no such situation. Remember, successfully meeting girls is largely a learned skill—the more you meet and talk to, the better you'll be at it. Then, when someone comes along that really interests you, you'll be like an athlete who has trained and conditioned himself into top form.

Trying Too Hard

Believe it or not, trying too hard can be just as ineffective as inaction and procrastination. I'm not talking about guys who are obnoxious or egotistical. Often the men who try too hard are nice guys. They may have a good sense of humor and a great personality. So what's the problem?

The problem is that they're in too big of a hurry, usually as a result of being nervous or insecure. They try to push things along so rapidly that the girls they meet never get a chance to notice that they really are nice guys. Instead, girls feel pressured by the hurried pace and immediately go into defensive mode—drawing back, building up their walls, and saying no.

Here is a seemingly odd analogy that helps explain how a guy goes wrong when he tries to move too fast with a girl. In the early 1980's, large numbers of American corporations began a big push to establish business ties with powerful Japanese manufacturing firms. Suddenly, lots of U.S. firms that had never done business in Japan were sending their executives overseas to wrap up what they saw as mutually beneficial commercial deals. Many of these hard-driving Americans, inexperienced in Japanese ways, became impatient when Japanese executives seemed unwilling to get down to business. Sometimes they would be there for weeks, and still the Japanese would avoid any serious discussion of business matters.

In frustration, the Americans would very often force the issue. Refusing to be delayed any longer, they would insist on being heard. The Japanese, always polite, would usually agree and then listen quietly as the Americans made their presentations. Afterwards, the Americans would return home certain that they had made their cases well and that contracts or deals with the Japanese seemed very likely— but no contracts or deals ever came. Why not? The Americans had unknowingly violated Japanese cultural traditions.

In Japanese culture, you take time to get to know someone socially before you even consider entering into a business relationship. The Japanese businessman wants to know the people he deals with on a personal level. He wants to establish trust and good communication first. Consequently, before any business would be discussed with the Americans, the Japanese wanted to spend time with them on the golf course, at lunches and dinners, in nightclubs, etc.

This process of getting to know each other could take days, weeks, or even longer as far as the Japanese were concerned. They were in no hurry. To them, this was the most important part of the negotiation. To the Americans, however, it all seemed like a huge waste of time. They had come to Japan to cut deals, not to wander around golf courses. They simply didn't understand the cultural importance for the Japanese of establishing personal ties before establishing business ties.

How does all this relate to guys who try too hard and are in too big of a hurry when they meet a girl? In a sense, girls are like the Japanese—their priorities are different than ours. They don't want to be rushed. They are generally more cautious and emotionally oriented than we guys are, and contrary to what many men believe, they aren't as fixated on good looks. They want to spend time getting to know you and assessing what kind of person you are, and if you won't allow them an opportunity to do this, they're very likely to show you the door.

In the following situation, Barry has spotted a girl he thinks is attractive at a busy nightclub in the city.

Barry: Hi. You want to dance?
Laura: I'm kind of tired right now. I've been dancing for the last twenty minutes.
Barry: Come on, you can do one more dance. You're here to have a good time, right? Come on, let's dance.
Laura: Not right now. Maybe later.
Barry: Let me buy you a drink then.
Laura: No thanks.
Barry: Why not? Hey, if you don't drink, I'll get you a soda, okay?
Laura: No, I'm fine.
Barry: You sure?
Laura: Yes! Look, I haven't finished the drink I've got.
Barry: Oh, yeah, sorry. Say, you want to dance in about

	fifteen minutes? You should be rested by then.
Laura:	Maybe…I don't know.
Barry:	Tell you what, I'll come back in fifteen minutes, and we can dance then, all right?
Laura:	I don't know, I…
Barry:	What's wrong?
Laura:	Look, I'm sorry, I just want to talk to my friends, okay?
Barry:	Sure, no problem, I'll just come back when you're ready. We can dance then.
Laura:	No, I don't want to dance. I just want to be with my friends.
Barry:	So I shouldn't come back?
Laura:	Right.

Barry probably could have saved this situation if he had realized that he was rushing Laura and stopped pressing so hard. She didn't really turn him down at first. She actually had been dancing for twenty minutes and probably was tired. Barry needed to back off with his requests and simply talk to her for a while, give her a little time to get to know him and get comfortable. After a short conversation, Laura probably would have agreed to dance. Instead, Barry kept the pressure on. Like a used-car salesman, he pushed her hard to sign on the dotted line. The more he pushed, the more she pulled back.

Paradoxically, although Barry's high-pressure advance seems confident on the surface, Laura reads it differently. To her, Barry looks weak and insecure. How's that? She perceives that Barry is in a big hurry because he doesn't have faith in his ability to charm and entertain her in a normal, casual conversation. He feels that he has to quickly push her into a commitment before she gets away.

She knows the truth, she can feel it—Barry is scared. He wants to get some kind of agreement from her (to dance, accept a drink, etc.) as quickly as possible so that he can relax and free himself of the fear that she will reject him. Unfortunately, it's all counterproductive. What Barry (and many guys) sees as gutsy, energetic behavior, Laura perceives as clumsy weakness that quickly begins to make her uncomfortable. This is not what girls respond to. They respond to confidence and a natural, easy approach that makes them feel like a person, not a hunted animal.

All that Barry needs is more experience talking and interacting with a variety of women. The more time he spends practicing his conversational skills, the more he will gain true confidence in his abilities with women. As his confidence and style grows, women will begin to respond more positively to him, and he will no longer feel the need to use hard-sell tactics on them.

I've spent a lot of time on this segment because Barry's errors are extremely common. They may in fact be the most common type of errors that guys make. You can't pressure a girl into wanting to be with you. You have to make her feel comfortable and then charm her.

Conversation Primer

Sometimes the mere thought of walking up to a completely unfamiliar female and trying to open and maintain a fascinating conversation—*cold*—can be pretty scary. How in the hell do you pull off such a trick? You've probably never seen the girl before in your life. You don't know diddley about her. She doesn't know doodley about you. So, how *do* you talk fluently to a total stranger?

Performing a feat like this with skill and style may seem like magic, but it isn't. Like most magic tricks, once you are shown the secrets, you realize that it wasn't really sorcery after all. Of course, while knowing the secrets of a trick may burst its mystery, it does not relieve you of the need to practice the methods of the trick until you can perform them seamlessly. The voodoo of knowing how to meet and charm a woman with words is really just two things. First, knowing the underlying secrets, which turn out to be fairly commonsense techniques, and second, practicing those techniques until your execution is so flawless that it seems downright mystical. Now, let's take a close look at the "secrets."

Whenever you approach a girl, think of yourself as

Sherlock Holmes. Like the great detective, you must use all your senses in the search for clues—clues that will reveal insights about her that you can discuss and questions about her that you can ask. The information you need to open and carry on a conversation will always be there, right in front of you. Don't worry that there might be times when there won't be any clues. Have faith. The clues will always be there—*always*. All you need to do is train yourself to look for them and recognize their potential.

Once you spot a girl that interests you, you use every moment to carefully observe her person, her behavior, her companions, and anything relevant in her surroundings or situation. Everything that you see and hear you will use to build a profile of observations that describe who she is, what's going on around her, and what questions about her need answers. All these things will become the raw materials you use to construct your conversation.

As you collect observations, you can employ them to start and maintain *conversational chains*. The following quotation from my other book on meeting women, *50 Secrets of Picking Up Girls* explains this view of how talk between people works—

> A conversation can be thought of as a long chain made up of ideas and subjects that are its links. Each new conversational link is logically connected to the previous link. For example, if the girl with whom you are speaking says, "I own a horse," the word *horse* is the link to which you attach the next link. Only a conversational amateur would respond to this statement by saying, "Oh, no kid-

ding, that's great." A response like this breaks the chain of conversation by failing to attach anything of substance to her statement. Instead, you should keep the talk moving forward by attaching a link that is relevant to *horse*. You do this by asking or commenting in some material way about that topic—"Where do you keep your horse?" If she then says, "I keep him up at the Jackson Canyon stables," you can now use either *Jackson Canyon* or *stables* as new links to hook onto—"I'll bet there are lots of great riding trails up around Jackson Canyon."

Understanding these basic rules of conversation makes it far easier to keep the talk progressing naturally, even under difficult circumstances. Of course, while conversational chains describe how normal smooth-flowing talk often works, there is room for creativity and variation in any conversation. You don't have to follow conversational chains unswervingly. You can always change the subject, veer off sharply, or hark back to earlier statements, etc.

Okay, now that you have searched for clues to use in opening and maintaining a conversation, it's time to consider managing the direction of the discussion. If you are a guy who is truly skilled in the art of meeting women, you don't just talk aimlessly, passing the time with any old subject that comes along. It may be fine to let the talk drift on the verbal wind when you are chatting with your great aunt Matilda, but tonight you are looking for romance. When you meet the girl of your dreams, you want to create some fire, and that means you need to actively seek out subjects that have the potential to throw off sparks.

Teach yourself to focus your conversation, to send it down the paths you want it to go. When getting to know a woman, always keep an eye out for the sensual or emotional angles of any given topic. In addition, probe for the ideas and subjects that she is passionate about, anything that she finds exciting. Also, stay alert for ideas, opinions, and life experiences that the two of you have in common. All of these elements will supercharge your talk, making you seem more interesting, exciting, and attractive. If the conversation doesn't go in these directions on its own, then you have to grab the wheel and steer it to the destination you desire.

Our next pick-up artiste, Tom, is an expert conversation detective and architect. He is always tuned in to what is going on around him and what is unique or noteworthy about the people he meets. Watch how he builds a conversation from the limited material that is available in the next dialog, and then, once he has the talk rolling, watch how he begins to mold the shape of the talk to his needs.

In the following lunchtime encounter at a local college, Tom has just gone through the cafeteria line and is now looking for a place to set down his tray and eat. As he wanders among the crowded tables, he spots a pretty blond sitting by herself reading a woman's glamour magazine.

Tom: Twelve ways to drive your lover mad with desire.
Barb: (small frown) What did you say?
Tom: (grins and points) The cover of your magazine.

	The headline says, "Twelve Ways to Drive Your Lover Mad with Desire." I've got to know if you think they'll work.
Barb:	(smiles slightly) I don't know. I haven't read that article yet.
Tom:	Saving the best part for last, huh?
Barb:	(smiles) Actually, I'm not sure I would want to drive a lover to madness.
Tom:	Hmm, good point. Do you mind if I sit here? It's kind of crowded today.
Barb:	(glances around the room) Sure, I guess so.
Tom:	(puts his tray down and sits) Tell me if I've got this right—you've finished your morning classes and now you're stuck here for a long layover until a late afternoon class starts.
Barb:	(smiles broadly) How did you know that?
Tom:	Oh, well, you've got your book bag stored under your chair, you've finished your lunch, and you're just sitting here reading a magazine that's got nothing to do with school. You look like a person who's settling in for a long wait.
Barb:	You're right, I am. Very observant.
Tom:	Thanks. I've been there, last quarter. Almost a four-hour wait. I was so bored that I always had to fight the temptation to blow off my afternoon class.
Barb:	Oh, I know! But I can't do that, this class is too important.
Tom:	What class is it?
Barb:	Biology.

Tom:	Ahh, biology. Well, for a class like that, maybe you ought to study up on those twelve ways to drive your lover mad with desire. That sounds like some serious biology to me.
Barb:	(laughs) We're studying Nematoda worms today.
Tom:	Whoa, I doubt there are twelve ways for a worm to be driven mad with desire.
Barb:	(giggling) I'm not sure it's possible for a worm to be driven mad, period. What would a crazy worm be like anyway?
Tom:	Only a worm psychiatrist could answer that.
Barb:	Oh, please, don't get me started on this! My sense of humor can get kind of bizarre. At least that's what my friends say.
Tom:	Hey, worm mental health is no laughing matter. All right, all right, I'll let you off, but only if you give me an example of your humor, something that your friends thought was bizarre.
Barb:	Ohhh nooo!
Tom:	Come on, just one little example.
Barb:	Okay, just one...no I can't.
Tom:	Come on, just one. I won't think badly of you. I'm a little nuts myself, really.
Barb:	Well, okay. Once my friends and I were driving past a hotel down by the beach and there was this guy...I can't believe I'm telling you this, you're going to think I'm a complete weirdo.
Tom:	No, I won't, I promise.
Barb:	Well, this guy was standing out on the deck of

	his room completely naked. Showin' it off for all the world to see, you know.
Tom:	Yeah.
Barb:	So I told my friends to drive back around so we could go by this nutball again, and then I leaned out the window and flashed him, you know, boobs.
Tom:	You are a complete weirdo.
Barb:	(laughs excitedly) Hey! You promised.
Tom:	Okay, okay, sorry. So what did the guy do?
Barb:	He waved—his hand, and his you know what.
Tom:	Do you suppose flashing is one of the twelve ways to drive a man mad with desire?
Barb:	It sure worked on that guy.
Tom:	You are a piece of work, young lady.
Barb:	Thank you
Tom:	Let me ask you something else. (he reaches out and takes one of Barb's hands into his own) What do your friends think of your very unique, artistic fingernails? (each of Barb's fingernails has a small picture or design painted on it)
Barb:	Oh, I do them like that when I'm bored. My friends think they're kind of cool. My girlfriends are always after me to do theirs. If you'd come along a little later, you might have caught me painting them.
Tom:	Very nice. What's this one? It looks kind of like a blue worm driven mad with desire.
Barb:	(laughs) Oh stop. It's actually a graph of the ups and downs of my grade point average over the

last two years.
Tom: No way! You're kidding me...aren't you?
Barb: Yes.

Tom is pretty effective here. Within this seemingly relaxed, playful conversation, Tom is actually performing a number of well-practiced techniques. Because he is so skilled and confident, Barb quickly gets into their conversation, even though she hadn't been all that receptive at first. And that's the point—the more polished your conversation skills are, the easier you make it for the girl to respond positively.

None of this should imply, however, that you must endure a burden of tiresome concentration and calculation in order to make your talk smooth and interesting to others. On the contrary, a skilled conversationalist like Tom has practiced his methods until they are almost second nature, and consequently, he enjoys himself just as much as his partner does. Now let's look at some of the details of Tom's encounter with Barb.

Note that Tom doesn't simply walk up to Barb and ask her straightaway if he can sit with her. Instead, he first makes an effort to get her attention and interest. He does this by quickly surveying the girl and everything in her immediate surroundings until he finds something entertaining to comment on, in this case, her magazine's racy headline—"Twelve Ways to Drive Your Lover Mad with Desire." Initially, Barb is a little annoyed to be bothered, but Tom's opener is too offbeat to ignore—she's interested despite herself. Having gotten the door open wide enough to get permission to sit, Tom now clinches the deal with another observation—Barb must be suffering through a long wait between classes. He sympathizes, tells her that he too has had that problem, and then reveals how he felt about it and responded to it.

All the while, Tom keeps the conversational chain from being broken by consistently responding in a meaningful way to whatever Barb says or has previously said. He also subtly guides the direction of the conversation's content, keeping it light, mildly erotic, and focused on Barb. He is so successful at this that Barb is soon quite relaxed and swept up in the discussion's flirtatious give and take. Even though Tom is almost a total stranger, she finds herself revealing a story about flashing her boobs in public.

Finally, she confirms that Tom has charmed her when she slyly teases him with a ludicrous little lie about the meaning of one of her fingernail designs. This is a good indicator to keep in mind—when a girl starts playing with you in this way, she likes you.

Opportunity Knocks

Tim and Jack have stationed themselves along a heavily trafficked aisle in a local club. Approaching them are two girls who are talking to each other excitedly and laughing loudly. As the girls pass by, Tim reaches out and takes one of the girls gently by the hand.

Tim: Hey, wait a minute! (smiling) You girls are having too much fun. What's going on here?

Allison: It's girl's night out. We're supposed to have fun.

Jack: Well, we're here to have fun too. We think you should hang out with us until we get to the bottom of this.

Tim: Right! We're the good-times police. We have to check you girls out, just to make sure there's no violations going on.

Geena: Oh, Mr. Officer, we promise to be good!

Jack: You hear that, Officer Tim? These girls promise to be good. I like it.

Allison: Hey, *I* didn't promise to be good. I might be good, but maybe I'll be bad.

Tim: Hmm, that doesn't sound like a violation to me.

Here is the awesomely revealing companion book to *Conversations*. The 50 most essential rules for capturing the opposite sex. Read it, or weep.

It's no secret that women are different from men, but few guys understand how to shape their conversation and behavior to use those differences to their advantage. Instead, they make age-old errors and never understand why their efforts fail.

Why does a girl choose one guy and pass on the next? Is it good looks? Sometimes, but far less often than you'd think. Ordinary guys can have extraordinary success with girls when they know what to do. It truly isn't that difficult; it just appears mysterious until you learn the secrets.

This book is a tool, a manual for reprogramming your approach to the opposite sex. Here are the rules you need to know—all laid out in these pages with clear explanations and lots of examples.

Stop staring at beautiful, intriguing women and start meeting them and making them a part of your life. —106 pages

ORDER NOW
from ***THINGS YOU NEVER KNEW EXISTED...***
Call **1-800-588-1142** (open 24 hours) and ask for **Item 5656—*50 Secrets of Picking Up Girls***
OR
Go to **www.johnsonsmith.com** and type **5656** in the Quick Search box.

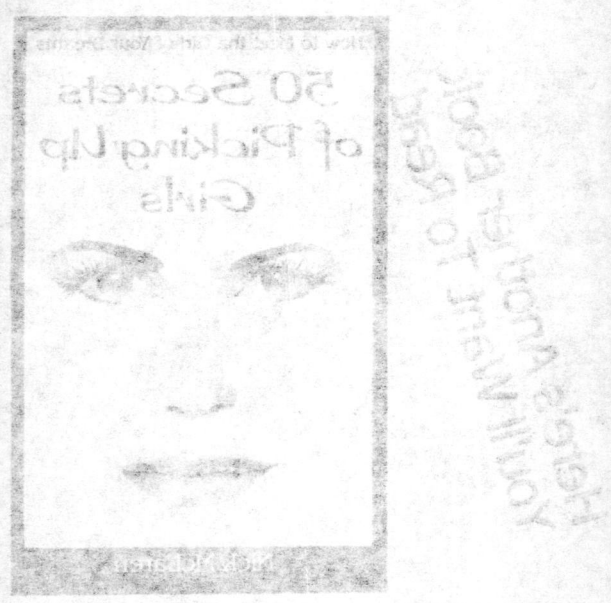

Here's a Book You Won't Want To Put Down

	What do you think, Jack?
Jack:	Definitely not. Why don't you girls let us buy you a drink? Then we'll find out who wants to be good and who wants to be bad.
Allison:	(After some quick eye contact with Geena) Well, okay, but only because you're the "police."
Tim:	We're just doing our job, sweetheart.

No guts, no glory. Jack and Tim did a masterful job of seizing an opportunity on a moments notice. They didn't analyze the situation to death, they didn't think too much, they acted. Tim recognized the girl's loud laughter as an opening for conversation, Jack immediately followed through, and they both quickly developed a humorous theme (the good-times police) to build conversation around and to project an image as fun loving guys.

These two girls are obviously out to have a good time, and they quickly realized that Jack and Tim were going to entertain them and be fun to hang out with. The key point here—most guys would have been intimidated by the girl's close conversation and spirited laughter, but Tim saw it as a chance to make contact. In the end, what impresses the girls is the self-confidence and ease with which these two guys handle themselves.

With Friends Like This...

In the previous encounter, Jack and Tim made a good team. This isn't always the case. Friends can help, but they can also hurt by embarrassing you or bringing up subjects that aren't smart to get into. Often a friend's errors are unintentional, but it isn't unheard of for a friend, even a close friend, to screw things up for you on purpose. He may not like the idea of you walking away with a great looking girl. Maybe he wants her for himself, or maybe he just doesn't want to be left alone if you hook up with an available female.

In the following situation, Mark is doing his best to meet and make a good impression with Sandra, but his partner Jimmy keeps shooting him down. It's hard to say whether Jimmy is just conversationally inept or is intentionally trying to ruin Mark's chances.

Mark: Jimmy, see that girl over there? What do you think?
Jimmy: She's okay.
Mark: Okay! She's fantastic! I think she's alone too.
Jimmy: So go talk to her, big dog.

Mark: I am. You coming?
Jimmy: Wouldn't miss it.
Mark: (walks over to the girl with Jimmy) Hi, if you're not expecting someone, we thought we'd keep you company for a while.
Sandra: (smiles) I'm just waiting for my girlfriend. She's always late.
Jimmy: She good lookin'?
Sandra: I think so.
Jimmy: Women always think their girlfriends are good lookin', even if they're total dogs.
Mark: Jimmy, lighten up, man. (to Sandra) Anyway, we just saw you standing here and thought you looked kind of lonely.
Jimmy: That's not what he told me (laughs).
Sandra: Oh really, what did he tell you?
Jimmy: Oh, just that he'd like to be the father of your children.
Mark: Jimmy! (then to Sandra) He's just giving me a bad time. I didn't say that.
Jimmy: (laughs) Not much.
Mark: Don't pay any attention to him.
Sandra: I'm trying not to.
Mark: So, you and your late friend are out for the night, huh?
Sandra: Uh-huh.
Jimmy: You two got boyfriends?
Mark: Jimmy!
Jimmy: Hey, I'm just trying to find out if we're wasting our time.

Sandra:	Yes, we both have boyfriends.
Jimmy:	(to Mark) There you are, man. We're wasting our time.
Mark:	Well, uh, we'll just hang out with you until your girlfriend gets here.
Sandra:	That's okay, you don't need to. Oh, that's her now! Listen, I have to go. Nice meeting you (turns and walks rapidly away).
Mark:	Way to go, Jimmy.
Jimmy:	She was a bitch. Who needs her.

Mark would do well to leave Jimmy at home the next time he wants to meet girls. Jimmy is a walking liability. When you are with a guy like Jimmy, you can't escape guilt by association. In a situation like this, whatever your friends say reflects on you. The girl doesn't know you. She can't really separate you from your friends. Basically, she'll use whatever information is available to make a judgment about you. That information includes the actions and words of the people who are with you.

In the first thirty minutes or so after meeting a girl, what comes out of your friends' mouths might as well come out of yours. Of course, after she gets to know you better as an individual, the way your friends act will have less and less influence on her opinion of you. But at first, you *are* your friends. So, if they are going to drag you down, don't hesitate to work alone. Don't cling to them for security, and don't stay with them just to be keep them happy.

He Who Hesitates Is Lost

In our next situation, Gary is about to get himself into trouble at a dance club. He has been eyeing a girl for about fifteen minutes but hasn't gotten up the nerve to talk to her. Hoping that getting close to her will help solve his confidence problem, he goes and stands next to her at a low wall overlooking the dance floor. Instead of starting a conversation, however, he just stands there, glancing sideways at her every once in a while.

After about five minutes, he apparently loses his nerve and steps away. Circling the room, he stops on the far side and stares at her, certain that she doesn't notice him watching her. After circling the room a few more times, he comes back to the wall and stands next to her again. She clearly knows that he's been watching her, but Gary doesn't seem to realize it. After a few more minutes pass, Gary finally gathers his courage and speaks.

Gary: Uh, hi. Want to dance?
Trudy: No.
Gary: Oh, sure, no problem. Crappy band, huh?

Trudy: That's my brother's band.
Gary: Oh, sorry. I, uh…they're not that bad. It's, uh, it's just that the acoustics are pretty bad in here. Sorry, I didn't mean to insult your brother.
Trudy: (Says nothing and stares straight ahead)
Gary: So, I guess you come here pretty often, um, since your brother plays here and everything?
Trudy: No.
Gary: You mean you don't go see your brother play very often?
Trudy: Yes, I do! I haven't been here before because this is the first time he's played here. Now, would you just leave me alone.
Gary: What's wrong with you? I only asked you a question. Aw forget it!
Trudy: I will, the minute you leave.

Oops! Gary made more mistakes here than even the most tolerant girl would stand for. First, he's so slow to act that before he even opens his mouth, Trudy is convinced that he's a weirdo. All of his indecision, sneaking around, and shifty-eyed glances have not gone unnoticed. She knows he's there, and he's making her uncomfortable. No girl wants to be with someone that makes her uncomfortable. Furthermore, this behavior tips her off that he has no self-confidence. It makes him seem weak, and girls don't like weakness.

Gary's second big error is to say something negative—the band is "crappy". It's always risky to say something negative when you've just met someone. A guy who is full of complaints doesn't seem like a fun person to be with. In addition, you never know when a negative statement is going to backfire. Even if the band hadn't been her brother's, Trudy still might have thought it was great.

Finally, Gary insults her with a statement that seems to imply that she doesn't support her brother's career by going to hear him play. This was just plain bad judgment. How could he expect her not to be insulted? The sad part is that he probably says all these things out of sheer nervousness. He may not actually believe that the band is "crappy" or that Trudy wasn't being good to her brother—he is just desperately trying to find something to say.

It's hard to rescue yourself after a bad beginning (spying on the poor girl for twenty minutes). A good opening line might have helped—"You know, I've checked out this whole place, and you're the best looking girl here. If you'll dance with me just once, I'll figure my whole night was a success." This might have saved him, but in all likelihood his work here was done before it started.

The worst part is that Gary obviously never quite figured out what the problem was. Instead of understanding that his approach was to blame, he may damage his ego even further by assuming that she didn't like him because of his looks or basic personality.

Spontaneous Combustion

John and Mike have just entered a busy upscale bar down by the beach. As they make their way through the crowd, one of the cocktail girls moves ahead of them and then stops to drop off a couple of colorful drinks at a booth occupied by two stunning blondes. John and Mike pause, waiting for the cocktail girl to finish so they can order some drinks for themselves. After a moment, the girl turns to them and asks for their order.

John: You know, I'm not sure what I want. (he addresses the two girls with the colorful drinks) What are you two drinking?

Tina: Piña Coladas. (grins mischievously) But they aren't the kind of drinks men usually have.

John: (laughs) That's where you're wrong. We're real men, but we're sensitive.

Mike: That's right, we're in touch with our feelings, our female side.

Shawna: I think you two are full of it (grins).

John: You may be right about that. (turns to the

	cocktail girl) Two Buds.
Tina:	So, I guess you're not really in touch with your female side?
Mike:	You've got us all wrong. We're sensitive as hell.
John:	It's just that right now we're more interested in your female side than ours.
Shawna:	(laughs) This is Tina, and I'm Shawna.
Mike	Mike (pointing to himself), and John.
Tina:	Nice to meet you. Do you live here?
Mike:	Born and raised.
Shawna:	You come in here to pick up on poor tourist girls like us?
John:	Nothing about either of you looks poor to us, right Mike?
Mike:	Nothing at all. I'll bet we have much more to fear from you than the other way around.
John:	That's right, you two probably go through men faster than the bartender can mix drinks.
Tina:	(laughs) You're horrible! We're very nice girls. Very nice girls!
Shawna:	(holds up her hand) But not *too* nice.
Mike:	That's music to my ears. Do you mind if we sit down and explore this in more detail? (Shawna and Tina grin at each other and then slide over to make room in their booth.)

Compare this meeting to the previous situation with Gary. John and Mike are totally spontaneous. John gets the girls talking in a very casual, offhand manner that puts everyone at ease. From that point until they finally ask the girls if they can join them, John and Mike keep the conversation on a light, humorous level with a little friction thrown in to spice things up.

Note that they totally avoid the usual list of boring questions that most guys end up asking in a forced effort to keep a conversation going. Questions such as—Do you come here often? Where do you work? Where do you go to school? Do you think this rain is ever going to stop? Blah, blah, blah. This type of interrogation may indeed keep a conversation from dying outright but only by putting it on life support. Talk like this is incredibly dull and doesn't communicate to a girl that you are a fun person to be with.

Note also the nice but subtle sexual tension that is maintained all through the above conversation. Tina was actually the one who initiated this pleasant tension when she implied that a Piña Colada wasn't the kind of drink a real man would order. John and Mike immediately picked up on this theme and used it to keep the conversation's interest and excitement level high. Compare their performance with the way the guy in the next situation handles his conversation.

Guts but No Glory

Jason has been hanging out with a couple of his buddies in the bar of a popular downtown restaurant. Across the room, he spots a girl sitting at a table with another girl and guy who are obviously a romantic couple. Her companions are deep in conversation, and the unattached girl is sitting there looking bored. Jason decides this offers a great opportunity to go and talk to her. He picks up his drink and strolls across the room to the girl.

Jason: Hi.
Linda: Hi.
Jason: I haven't seen you here before.
Linda: (shrugs)
Jason: Uh, so I guess this is your first time here, huh?
Linda: No, I've been here before.
Jason: Really, 'cause I haven't seen you before.
Linda: You said that.
Jason: Yeah, I guess I did (laughs nervously). So, you're here with your friends?
Linda: Uh-huh.
Jason: They boyfriend and girlfriend? (the "friends"

	happen to be kissing at that moment)
Linda:	You might say that.
Jason:	So why are you alone?
Linda:	(frowns) What?
Jason:	Never mind. Are you here to eat dinner?
Linda:	No, we just came by after work for a drink.
Jason:	Oh. Where do you work?
Linda:	A temp service.
Jason:	A temp service. What's that?
Linda:	We fill secretarial jobs temporarily for local businesses that need extra help.
Jason:	Sounds kind of boring. (laughs)
Linda:	I own the business. It's not boring at all.
Jason:	Oh, hey, sorry. That was a stupid thing to say.
Linda:	Listen, I have to go. (turns to her friends) I have to leave. It's late.
Jason:	So, uh, maybe we can go out some time. Why don't you give me your phone number?
Linda:	I don't give out my phone number.

Boring! Still, you have to give poor Jason some credit. He did have the guts to approach this girl cold, he hung in there during a conversation that wasn't going well, and he threw caution to the wind and asked her out, even though he must have known it was a lost cause.

We can give him a good grade for guts, but a failing grade for technique. What was the basic problem that Jason had to solve in order to be successful?

First, he needed to analyze the situation before he stepped into it. Linda's problem here is that she is out with two people who aren't paying much attention to her. The couple she is with are romantically wrapped up with each other, leaving Linda bored and probably a little gloomy.

Second, Jason needed to develop a plan for solving Linda's predicament. If he had found a way to entertain her, to lift her spirits and make her laugh, he would have made a far better impression. Unfortunately, this was not what he did. Instead, he burdened Linda even further with a long string of dull, lifeless questions that only increased her boredom and blues.

What could Jason have done to make a positive impression? This situation called for action that was imaginative and even surprising. It required something that would shake things up and give Linda reason to believe that there might be possibilities for this night after all. Consider what might have happened if Jason had first approached the romantic couple sitting with Linda and said (with a smile), "Excuse me, I know you two don't realize it, but you're so in love with each other that I think your poor friend here feels forgotten."

This is a gutsy, ingenious approach, something different, something that would intrigue Linda. Her two friends, after a moment of shock, would undoubtedly laugh and then heap apologies on Linda. Now, the couple would probably join the conversation, taking some of the pressure to keep things going off of Jason. And best of all, Linda would probably feel that Jason had rescued her from an unpleasant evening.

Down on Me

Sam has been talking to Michelle for about ten minutes at a party being held at the house of mutual friends. Michelle knows that Sam is close to the married couple who are throwing the party. Because she trusts these people, she also trusts that Sam is a good guy. Translation—Sam has a leg up here. He doesn't have to prove himself as much as the guy who approaches a girl in a bar and has no one to recommend him. The question is, what will Sam do with this advantage?

Michelle: So, what do you do, Sam?
Sam: (laughs) For a living?
Michelle: Yes. I'll bet you're a firefighter.
Sam: A firefighter! What makes you think that?
Michelle: I don't know, you just have that look.
Sam: Naw, I'm a runt compared to most firefighters. I wish I was. That'd be a great job compared to what I do.
Michelle: (pause) Well?
Sam: Well what?
Michelle: What do you do?

Sam:	Oh, sorry! Not much. I'm a salesman for a fine linens manufacturer. But it's not what I ought to be doing.
Michelle:	What do you mean? What should you be doing?
Sam:	It's a crummy job. If someone had told me ten years ago that I'd be doing this, I never would have believed it.
Michelle:	It doesn't sound so bad to me.
Sam:	Aw, maybe it doesn't, but it is. At my age I should be thinking of buying a house, instead I'm just praying that my piece of junk car will hold together for another year.
Michelle:	Uh-huh.
Sam:	Funny that you'd think I was a firefighter.
Michelle:	Why?
Sam:	Well, I've got an older brother who's a firefighter.
Michelle:	Really?
Sam:	Yeah, he's doing great. I'd be happy if I was doing half as well as him. You may not know it, but it's tough to become a firefighter. They have to pass a lot of physical and educational tests. I never could have done it.
Michelle:	Sure you could!
Sam:	Naw, I don't think so.

Sam sure knows how to throw away a good thing. Here he's been introduced to a beautiful example of the opposite sex, and he spends all his time convincing her that he's a loser. More importantly, in this case he succeeded. Michelle moved on shortly after this. And why not? Sam is negative. He's convinced that he's a nobody, and he's not shy about saying so.

Michelle gives Sam numerous opportunities to be positive about himself, and he ignores every chance. What is she to think? What reason has he given her to stick with him or to develop an interest in him? He's all gloom and doom. He sounds like the kind of person who eventually drags down anyone who spends enough time around him. Worst of all, after Michelle left, he probably concluded that she didn't like him because of his looks.

The Anywhere Man

Don't forget that it's possible to meet females anywhere. You don't have to wait until you're in a bar or at a party to talk to a woman you don't know. In the following situation, Rick has spotted a very pretty brunette who is looking over a bin of peaches at a local grocery store.

Rick: Are those any good?
Susan: Excuse me?
Rick: The peaches. Are they any good? I can never tell. I get them home and nine times out of ten they aren't ripe, they never get ripe, and they don't have a bit of flavor.
Susan: That is a problem. I end up throwing out quite a few myself.
Rick: Same with me! I'll bet I've thrown out enough peaches to fill up my kitchen to the countertops.
Susan: (laughs) Well, my luck with peaches hasn't been that bad.
Rick: That's because you know the secrets of peach purchasing. I recognized it immediately. She's a great peach purchaser, I said to myself. Maybe

	she can tell me the secrets, and then I can be a great peach purchaser.
Susan:	And stop throwing out kitchen loads of peaches.
Rick:	Absolutely!
Susan:	(laughs)
Rick:	So?
Susan:	So?
Rick:	Are these peaches any good?
Susan:	I have no idea.
Rick:	(laughs) You know something, I like you. If you're not attached, maybe you'd consider having some coffee with me…after we've gotten our groceries safely put away at home, that is.
Susan:	Maybe. You're not a loony are you?
Rick:	No way. I'm known far and wide for my sanity.
Susan:	I could do coffee in half an hour.
Rick:	Great. Maybe we can get some peach pie too.
Susan:	(laughs) We'll let someone else figure out if the peaches are good or not.

    Sometimes the best place to meet girls is the one you'd least expect. And often, because you don't think of it as a place to approach a girl, you don't. And because you don't, maybe you never meet the girl of your dreams.

    Rick does very well in the above meeting. One thing that isn't apparent from the text of the conversation is that Rick smiled a lot and maintained good eye contact (not an unbroken stare) all through his talk with Susan. This made him appear at ease and confident, even if he was a little nervous at first. It's a strange thing, but if you act confident, it isn't long before you feel confident.

Also, notice how quickly Rick involves Susan in a perfectly natural conversation. He keeps it light, and he gets her to start joking around, which increases her comfort level. And best of all, he never seems to be blatantly hitting on her, even though they both know he is. On the surface, he's just a friendly guy who isn't sure how to select peaches. Only after he has established that he is a funny, easy to get along with person does he ask her to have coffee.

There's little doubt that a less subtle approach can also work. If you charge up to enough girls and blurt out something like "You're the most beautiful girl I've ever seen! I just had to talk to you," it is true that you'll find a few who'll respond positively—but not many. With most girls, it's best to establish some trust and common ground before you make your big move.

An Attractive Offer

Here is another slightly unusual setting in which to meet a girl. Bob often drops in at a local coffee shop to get a sweet roll and a good cup of coffee before he heads off to work. For several weeks, he has noticed an attractive redhead who also seems to drop in for a pre-work coffee at about the same time he does.

The coffee shop has an outdoor patio with tables where the redhead generally sits while she sips her coffee and looks over the morning newspaper. Bob has decided that on this day he will do more than just check her out from a distance. Out on the patio, he selects a table next to the one occupied by the redhead.

Bob: You must be hooked on caffeine like I am.
Tina: (looks up from her newspaper) Excuse me?
Bob: I said you must be hooked on caffeine like I am. I see you in here ordering coffee just about every morning.
Tina: Couldn't hold down a job without it.
Bob: Me either. I suppose that if the coffee crop was wiped out, we wouldn't be able to make a living.

Tina:	(smiles) Scary, huh?
Bob:	No kidding. (pauses) I also think you have a secret desire to go to Hawaii.
Tina:	(laughs) Hawaii?
Bob:	Yeah, you always order Kona coffee. Like the Kona Coast in Hawaii. Admit it, you would rather be in Hawaii.
Tina:	Well, yes, but who wouldn't?
Bob:	Okay, so it's not such a brilliant observation.
Tina:	You sound like you know something about Hawaii yourself.
Bob:	A little bit. I spent about a month on the Kona Coast last summer.
Tina:	Really! Was it beautiful?
Bob:	Just like they say, paradise.
Tina:	I may drink Kona coffee, but I'm no expert on the Islands. Isn't Kona on the big island?
Bob:	Right. Western shore. I think you really do have a secret desire to go to Hawaii.
Tina:	I've always wanted to go but—
Bob:	The coffee is as close as you've gotten.
Tina:	That's it.
Bob:	If you'll allow me to move my coffee over to your table, I'll tell you exactly what Kona is like. When I'm done, you'll be so motivated, you'll find a way to get there no matter what.
Tina:	(laughs) Well...okay. You don't happen to work for a travel agency, do you?

Pretty well done. Bob hooks her with a comment about

caffeine that piques her interest, follows up with some easygoing humor, and then gets lucky with a stab in the dark about Hawaii. Hawaii is a great choice for conversation. What girl isn't going to want to talk about Hawaii? Even if he hadn't been there, it would be a great choice. They'd still have a great time talking about their mutual desire to go there on a dream vacation. It's always wise to initially talk about something attractive.

In the early part of any meeting, try not to get sidetracked on some negative, unpleasant subject like her breakup with a former boyfriend or the transmission problem she's having with her car. Talk about something fun or exciting, and let some of that fun and excitement rub off on you.

Finally, note how Bob uses a small bribe to persuade Tina to let him join her—namely, a full report on his wonderful, one-month vacation on the Kona coast. Better to offer her an enticement rather than just say, "Can I come sit with you?" After all, most girls are a little reluctant to allow a stranger into their space and life.

Mother Knows Best

Looking for a challenge? How about trying to pick up a girl who is out with her mother? Ryan is sitting with a buddy in a restaurant bar down at the harbor. Looking up, he is stunned to see a girl who he immediately describes to his friend as "just my type."

The girl is with an older woman, and the two sit down a couple of tables away. They are close enough that Ryan can hear a little of their conversation. It soon becomes clear that they are mother and daughter. After a few minutes, Ryan tells his friend that he is going over to talk to them. The friend is amazed and tries to talk him out of it, but Ryan insists and goes over to the women's table.

Ryan: (to the girl) Uh, listen, I know this is weird, but you are the prettiest girl I've ever see and...I'm real sorry to interrupt, really, but I just had to come over and talk to you.
Kelly: Oh God!
Mother: (to Ryan) She is pretty, isn't she?
Kelly: Mom!
Ryan: Yes, ma'am, she is.

Mother: Why don't you sit down and talk for a while?
Kelly: Mom!
Mother: Kelly, he thinks you're the prettiest girl he's ever seen. That's quite a compliment. We ought to at least ask him to stay awhile.
Ryan: (smiles) Thank you, don't mind if I do. (sits down quickly) I'm Ryan.
Mother: This is Kelly and I'm Carol.
Ryan: Nice to meet you.
Mother: Well, you seem like a nice young man. Are you?
Ryan: Yes, if you don't count the car I stole to get here.
Kelly: (laughs when her mother's eyes go wide) You asked him, Mom.
Ryan: I'm only kidding, and I've got the car payments to prove it. (to Kelly) You've got a nice laugh.
Kelly: Thanks.
Ryan: Look, I really am sorry if I'm interrupting anything.
Kelly: You should've thought of that before you came over here. But maybe this is a good thing.
Ryan: Really?
Mother: Yes, really.
Kelly: Maybe with you here, my mother won't do what she usually does.
Mother: Hey!
Ryan: What's that? Should I ask?
Kelly: Criticize.
Ryan: (winks at the mother) Oh yeah, I've had a little experience there myself.
Mother: Ryan, try to remember who got you the seat

	you're in. You ought to wait at least five minutes before you turn against me.
Ryan:	You're right, I apologize.
Kelly:	Wait a minute. I want to hear more about your criticizing mother.

As it turned out, Kelly had a boyfriend, but that doesn't make Ryan's ballsy move any less inspiring. He took his best shot (despite an opening line that isn't usually recommended). Things don't always work out, but if you don't try, it absolutely no way is going to work out. Even a 1% chance of success is better than 0%.

Also, consider one other fact. The element of this situation that seemed most threatening—the presence of the girl's mother—turned out to be the very element that got Ryan his seat next to Kelly. What's the point? Don't prejudge a situation. Don't overanalyze it. You *never* really know how an encounter is going to play out.

What a Joke

A sense of humor and sex appeal go hand in hand. Laughter makes a girl relax, and before long, it can turn her on. Most of us understand this and do our best to make girls laugh. The only problem is that it's very easy to get carried away with a joke and inadvertently reveal something unattractive about yourself, or worse, insult the girl you're trying to impress. These are astonishingly easy errors to make. They are the kind of misjudgments that leave you slapping your forehead and muttering, "Why did I say that? What an idiot!"

In this next conversation, Dave starts out well with Carrie, but then...

Dave:	Excuse me. Aren't you Carrie Miller?
Carrie:	Yes.
Dave:	You don't really know me, but I used to hang out with your brother Bill in high school. You look so much like him I thought you had to be the sister he used to talk about. I'm Dave Bryan.
Carrie:	(smiles) Oh, yeah, I've heard your name before. Did you ever come over to our house?
Dave:	No, I don't think so. Bill and I knew each other

	pretty well, but I don't think I ever went over to your house.
Carrie:	We've probably never met then. You must have graduated by the time I got to high school.
Dave:	Yeah, I think so. What's Bill doing these days?
Carrie:	He's doing well. He graduated from college about two years ago and works for an accounting firm in San Diego.
Dave:	He always did real well in school. I figured he'd be a success.
Carrie:	Yeah, he's a good guy. We're pretty close.
Dave:	Maybe you can give me his number. I'd like to see him again.
Carrie:	Sure, no problem. I'm sure he'd like to see you too.
Dave:	You know, I did see him a couple years ago down at the mall. He was on the opposite side of that upper level, and I couldn't get over to him, so we never actually talked.
Carrie:	Really.
Dave:	Yeah, the funny thing is that he was with this fat girl. I'm talkin' big time fat. I thought, poooor Bill. This girl was a hippo escapee from the zoo.
Carrie:	(after a pause) That was probably me. I worked at the mall for a while.
Dave:	Oh no, no, she was huge, really huge. It wasn't you. You look great.
Carrie:	I've lost almost 65 pounds in the last two years. It was me.

Disasters like this happen all the time. Unlike Dave, you'll often never find out where you went wrong because the girl won't tell you. All you'll ever know is that for some reason she didn't go for you.

It's probably impossible to avoid all such mistakes; there are just too many ways to go wrong when you're dealing with a person you don't know. However, you can reduce your risk if you keep your negative, sarcastic, mocking jokes to a minimum when you first meet someone. I'm not saying these types of jokes can't be funny. They are often hilarious. But, generally speaking, this kind of humor is appreciated more by guys than by girls, and it carries an increased risk of inadvertently insulting something the girl thinks is important.

Missed Signals

Whenever you meet a girl that you're attracted to, you are a salesman. What are you selling? Yourself. Seems simple, but lots of guys don't get it. They're negative, they put themselves down, they complain, they talk about how crappy their lives are, and not surprisingly, the girls are unimpressed. That's one extreme.

At the other extreme is the high-pressure guy who sells himself too hard. He is the oily, self-inflating huckster of the singles scene. It's certainly okay to build yourself up in the eyes of a girl, but subtlety is the key here. Most women (not all) are turned off by an arrogant and conceited jerk.

Kirt:	Hellll-o ladies. We want to talk to you!
Andy:	Yeah, you are definitely the girls of our dreams.
Mary:	No kidding.
Kirt:	Hell yes, no kidding. We only go for the fine stuff, and you two are the finest.
Mary:	You hear that, Tracy, we are "fine stuff."
Tracy:	Makes me feel all tingly.
Andy:	Makin' girls feel tingly is what me an' Kirt here are all about.

Mary:	Is that so?
Kirt:	Yes, it is.
Andy:	We saw you talkin' to those two losers earlier, and we decided to come over and save you, put some real excitement into your life.
Tracy:	Those other guys weren't losers.
Mary:	No, they weren't.
Andy:	Then where are they?
Kirt:	Who cares? At least you got rid of them. Why don't you—
Mary:	We didn't get rid of them. They had to leave.
Kirt:	I can't think of anything that'd make us leave two great lookin' babes like you.
Tracy:	Just our luck.
Andy:	You are in luck, sweetness. Why don't we get out of this dump? My partner here has a brand new BMW in the lot. Why don't you let us show you the town?
Mary:	We already know the town.
Andy:	Yeah, but you ain't seen it with us.
Kirt:	Seeing it with us is a whole new experience, baby, a whole new experience.
Andy:	We can buy you any kind of experience you want. Come on, let's get out of here.
Mary:	Pass.
Tracy:	We're waiting for some friends.
Kirt:	We'll wait with you.
Tracy:	My friend and I have some stuff to talk over.
Mary:	Private stuff.

Not all girls (but damn near) would have turned these guys down. There are always some who will go for the hard driving, self-puffers. The real problem here is that Kirt and Andy failed to read the signals. From the very beginning, these girls clearly were not buying their approach. They wanted subtlety and a slower pace, not bulldozers. Kirt and Andy blew right on past these signals and never slowed down until the girls showed them the exit. If they had been observant, they would have backed off early on and mellowed out. For these girls a more sophisticated approach was in order.

Staying Focused

Typically, when he meets a girl for the first time, a guy's focus is on what *he* is going to say. But consider this—when you meet a woman, how focused are you on what *she* is saying? One of the most effective ways to make a great impression on a girl is to listen well.

Generally speaking, guys do more talking than girls in any conversation. Another point, the next time you're in a conversation in which both guys and girls are present, pay attention to how often the guys cut the girls off in mid-sentence. Men frequently cut women off and do it so habitually that they aren't even aware of what they are doing. It's as if guys are so impatient that they just can't wait another second to express their thoughts. Or worse, they just don't think female opinions are worth hearing.

So, what's the point? The point is that lots of women feel that they rarely get the chance to fully express their ideas or feelings when they are with men. A guy who *does* give a woman a full hearing is going to seem special and different. However, this means more than just making an effort not to cut her off. It means that you really do listen closely to what she is saying and periodically indicate through a variety of techniques that you understand not only what she is saying but also how she feels (see "Six Basic Conversational Techniques" in *50 Secrets of Picking Up Girls*).

Women are far more preoccupied with emotions than guys are, which means you have to make an extra effort to focus on the feelings behind a woman's words. In the following situation, you'll meet a guy who is very skilled in this kind of "deep listening." (In the end, this situation works out well, but it could be argued that he makes a mistake by getting into an unpleasant subject. Judgment call.)

Greg: You seem kind of tired.
Christa: Oh, I probably am. I'm having kind of a hard time at work.
Greg: What's going on?
Christa: You don't want to hear about it. It's just a lot of depressing stuff.
Greg: I can take it. What's going on?
Christa: (smiles) Are you sure? I don't want to get you in a bad mood.
Greg: (smiles) We can be miserable together.
Christa: Well, it's just that I'm the secretary for three different managers at work. They all give me assignments, but none of them ever bothers to find out how much work the others have given me.
Greg: You have more work than you can do?
Christa: Right. I can't really tell any of them that I'm too busy to do what they want. They're all my bosses! So I keep getting further and further

behind, and they're coming at me all the time saying where's this and why haven't you done that. I just can't get it all done.

Greg: So, you're always under pressure, always feeling overwhelmed.

Christa: Yes! I feel guilty taking a break or even going to lunch because I know that when I come back, someone is going to be upset that something isn't finished and ready.

Greg: You probably feel like someone is going to jump out and start yelling at you at any moment.

Christa: That's exactly it! I kind of live in fear all the time. Lots of nights I can't even sleep worrying about who I'm going to have to face in the morning.

Greg: Don't any of these managers ever talk to each other? Don't they realize how much you're doing?

Christa: I don't know. I'm not sure they really care.

Greg: They just want their work done and don't care how you do it.

Christa: They aren't concerned with my problems.

Greg: What are you going to do?

Christa: I've tried to explain to them that I've got more work than I can do, or anyone could do, but it doesn't seem to have any effect. Now I think I'm going to have to go to the department head and explain the problem to him.

Greg: That's got to be pretty scary.

Christa: Oh yes, I'm scared to death. I keep putting it

	off, worrying about what will happen if things don't go well. I can't afford to lose my job.
Greg:	Christa, I'm sure they know you're a hard worker. Things will work out.
Christa:	Thanks, it does help just to talk about it. I didn't bore you did I?
Greg:	No way! I'm glad you felt you could talk it over with me.

This is a conversation the average guy would have screwed up. Notice that Greg doesn't interrupt to give her a lecture on how she should solve the problem. Notice also that his comments and questions tell her that he understands not only the facts of her predicament but also how she feels about them. He doesn't ask her about the details of the situation, instead he zeros in on how the problem must affect her emotionally. This really gives her the chance to express herself and to feel that she has been heard and sympathized with. Greg has made some major points with Christa. Very cool.

Open to a Fault

Most girls like a man who can be open about his feelings and needs, but there is such a thing as being too open. Often, guys who are lonely or just very aggressive about pursuing their goals can reveal so much of themselves that they scare girls off.

There is an old saying about the error of "putting the cart before the horse." If a cart is going to be pulled effectively, the horse has to come before the cart. When you meet a girl, there is a proper order for events to proceed. One step follows another. If you are too impatient and start putting the later steps first, you are going to have a problem.

After meeting at a friend's wedding reception, Ben gets a bit too open with Jennifer about his goals.

Ben: This has been a lot of fun. I'm glad I came.
Jennifer: I love weddings.
Ben: Are you married?
Jennifer: No.
Ben: Ever been married?
Jennifer: No, not even once.
Ben: Me either. Do you plan to get married?

Jennifer:	To the right guy.
Ben:	I had to break up with my last girlfriend. I wanted to get married, but she didn't.
Jennifer:	Uh-huh.
Ben:	How about kids, do you want kids?
Jennifer:	Sure, I—
Ben:	I want at least three kids, at least three. I've always wanted a big family.
Jennifer:	I come from a big family, three brothers.
Ben:	Really! That's great. I'm an only child. So, do you want lots of kids?
Jennifer:	Big families aren't always a picnic.
Ben:	Oh, I know that, I still want one anyway. But I have to get married first, right?
Jennifer:	Seems like the logical way to go.
Ben:	(laughs) Do you have a boyfriend?
Jennifer:	Not right now.
Ben:	Yeah, it's bad, not having someone. I'm not very good at being by myself. Some people are, you know. But not me, I like to be with people.
Jennifer:	Sure.
Ben:	You having trouble finding a good guy? Lots of girls complain about that. Most guys just aren't into commitment these days.
Jennifer:	I've met some good guys.
Ben:	Oh sure, they're out there, you just have to look. I'm into commitment myself. I want to get married and get my life going. You know what I mean?
Jennifer:	I think I do.

It seems pretty clear that even though they've barely talked for five minutes, Ben is evaluating Jennifer as a potential future wife. There's nothing wrong with that. The problem is that he's too obvious about it. Girls don't work this fast. He's driving way past her speed limit.

Girls don't jump easily from "Hi, how are you?" to the idea of matrimony. For them, a lot of things have to happen before they can even consider a relationship with a guy, much less marriage. To Jennifer, Ben's probing about marriage and kids probably seems ridiculous. How, she must wonder, can a guy who barely knows her name have the nerve to start evaluating her for marriage?

It's entirely possible that Ben and Jennifer might have made a great couple. They'll probably never find out. Ben blew it by putting the cart before the horse. He violated the female rules of order. He jumped from step 1 to step 15 without so much as a passing glance at steps 2 through 14. As a result, Jennifer is now uneasy and looking for a way out. A light conversation has turned into a pressure cooker.

Ben has clearly indicated that marriage and family are what drive him. If he asks her out, she knows that saying yes would practically be equivalent to agreeing to a thorough investigation of her marriageability, an obviously silly situation. Out of pure self-defense, she will say no if he asks.

Even if she were dying to get married, Ben's aggressive approach might still turn her off. The lesson? Don't operate at Ben's breakneck pace. Slow yourself down to the pace girls operate at, not the pace you'd like them to operate at. You may not want to go slow, but that's tough luck. Girls usually can't be successfully hurried.

Go for the Gold

Picking up a girl requires more than just maintaining a conversation. The object is to stir up some excitement, create some heat. In other words, go for the gold, don't just stand there and drone along about any subject that pops into your head. Speak with a purpose, act with a purpose.

Your job is to construct a conversation that does more than just occupy time. You want to entertain this girl, you want to make her laugh, and most of all, you want to turn her on. In the following conversation, Daryl and Jeff are at a nightclub and have been watching two girls who arrived a few minutes before. As the girls move toward them, Daryl overhears their conversation.

Holly:	It's so crowded.
Jean:	We'll never get a drink.
Daryl:	(stepping forward) Yes, you will.
Jean:	What?
Daryl:	We'll get you some drinks. (he then jumps up on his chair and yells to one of the cocktail girls over the heads of the crowd) PATTY! (when she looks, he waves her over)

Patty:	Yes, Daryl, your wish is my command.
Daryl:	Patty, you're my kind of girl. Marry me when you get off work (turns and winks at Jean).
Patty:	(speaking to Jean) He knows I'm already married. Daryl is such a bad boy.
Daryl:	Patty, these beautiful girls would like a drink.
Patty:	I think I can handle that. (she takes their order)
Jeff:	(hands Patty a $20) If they don't object, we'll buy the round.
Holly:	Thanks.
Jean:	Yes, thank you.
Jeff:	It's a pleasure.
Jean:	(to Daryl) You seem to be pretty well known around here. Is this a service you provide to all the women?
Daryl:	Absolutely not! Actually, we've never been here before in our lives. Right, Jeff?
Jeff:	That's right. People just warm up to us real quick.
Daryl:	Because we're so likable.
Holly:	So, if you've never been here before, how did Patty know your name, and why did she say that you knew she was married?
Daryl:	You know, I've been wondering about that myself.
Jean:	(laughs) Holly, I think these guys are a little crazy.
Holly:	A *little* crazy!
Jeff:	Beauty always makes us crazy.
Daryl:	Yep, we're suckers for beauty.

Holly: You mean us?
Daryl: I sure don't mean Jeff here.
Jean: They're good bullshitters, Holly, you can't deny that.
Jeff: You think we're good now, wait'll you've had a drink. You'll think you've gone to heaven.
Jean: Don't get carried away, Jeffrey.
Jeff: Oh, please! Don't say that, you sound like my mother.
Jean: (to Holly) Oh great! He's comparing me to his mother. That's sexy.
Jeff: On the other hand, my mother used to make me go to bed early when I was bad. You wouldn't consider that would you?"
Jean: Not yet.
Daryl: Ooooh, not yet!
Holly: (to Jean) Now you're getting carried away.
Daryl: Before we go any further, you know our names, but we don't know yours.
Holly: Maybe we like having you at a little disadvantage.
Daryl: Oh no, not fair.
Holly: Okay, I'm Holly and this is Jean.
Jeff: Beautiful names for beautiful ladies.
Jean: Uh-oh, there they go again.
Daryl: We can't help ourselves.
Holly: That's what we're afraid of.
Daryl: Holly, you don't seem like a person who's afraid of anything.
Jean: You got that right. It takes a hell of a guy to

	handle her.
Daryl:	(smiles and looks Holly in the eye) I love a challenge.

In case you haven't noticed, things are going well for Daryl and Jeff. Despite the kidding around and the seeming resistance, these girls like them. Daryl's first move, jumping up on a chair and calling the cocktail girl over, was very smart. For one thing, it solved the girls' problem—getting drinks in a jam-packed nightclub. More importantly though, it showed him to be an interesting man of action, a guy who pays attention to a girl's needs and does what has to be done to satisfy them. To a female, this is very romantic and sets him apart from the rest of the heedless, unconcerned, passive male pack.

Many guys just stand there when a girl expresses a need. Daryl, however, not only saw these girls' desire for a drink as an opening to start a conversation but also probably understood that it was a great way to make himself (and by association, Jeff) look very good. Smooth move.

Now look again at the content of the conversation. First, as we've said before, Daryl and Jeff don't waste time with a lot of boring questions about where the girls work or what the weather is like. Instead, their conversation is a game, a light give and take of exaggeration, purposefully uninhibited compliments, mild challenges, etc. The two girls quickly pick up on this, and the game is on. It's conversational friction, the kind that rubs all parties the right way.

This kind of easygoing but stimulating give and take is fun, it stirs everyone up, keeps them all on their toes. It's just the kind of experience most girls are looking for when they go out to have a good time. After a week of sitting behind a desk at work or in school, they want some excitement, some diversion, and this kind of conversation provides just that.

In addition, this verbal exchange involves some mutual testing by all the parties. The girls and the guys throw out mildly challenging comments and see how the other party handles them. It's a process of evaluating the other person's social skills, style, sense of humor, and especially, their sexual charisma. Meeting a girl and then saying, "Uh, so, do you come here often?" makes you about as entertaining as the computer she uses at work. Don't just fill time, show her a good time.

And a Little Embarrassment for Flavor

One of the most interesting ways of creating excitement and energy in a conversation is embarrassment. A little embarrassment can be very stimulating. Of course, I don't mean that you insult the girl or pull some dirty trick on her. That's not likely to win you any points. However, mild embarrassment that is the result of good-natured humor or stems from some error or minor peculiarity of the girl can be surprisingly arousing.

Careful though, don't create embarrassment that's linked to something the girl is likely to find painful. If she's a little overweight or doesn't have a perfect nose or has some other feature or characteristic that she's probably sensitive about, this is not a wise subject for jokes or embarrassment.

In the next segment, which takes place at a party, Paul uses embarrassment like a master. As he walks past a table occupied by two girls, one of them gestures wildly with her arm as she tells a story to her friend. Her hand swings out toward Paul, and although he could easily avoid it by stepping around, he instead blocks her forearm with his hand and grasps it.

Paul: Whoa! Watch out there.
Lynne: Oh, God. I'm so sorry. Did I hit you?
Paul: (still grasping her lower forearm, he slides his hand down and takes hold of her hand) You missed me this time, but I'm going to have to hold this hand until you've finished your story. (to Lynne's friend Katy) Is she always this dangerous?
Katy: She's pretty wild.
Lynne: (blushing) Oh, sorry! I forgot there are so many people around.
Paul: (still holding her hand) Is it safe to let go of your extremely nice hand?
Lynne: Yes, I think I can control myself now.
Paul: (holding up Lynne's hand but speaking to Katy) Look at these, long, slim fingers. This is the hand of a musician or an artist. Wouldn't you agree that this is an incredibly beautiful hand?
Katy: (laughs) Definitely. Why would she bash it around like a piece of wood?
Paul: I have no idea. It does seem like pretty strange behavior.
Lynne: (still blushing) Okay you two, leave me alone. I think both of you are starting to enjoy this a little too much.
Paul: (to Katy) Do you think we're enjoying this too much? That's a terrible accusation, don't you

	think?
Katy:	Yes, I do. You've been a perfect gentleman. All you've done is avoid her uncalled for attack and compliment her hands.
Lynne:	(to Katy) Traitor. (to Paul) Now, can I have my hand back?
Paul:	Yes, you may. But only if I can stand here and talk to you for a while.
Lynne:	Well, I guess that's the least I can do.
Paul:	Just try to be careful.
Lynne:	(laughs) I promise.

You can't help but believe that Lynne finds this whole situation embarrassing but also pleasantly stimulating. Note that Paul never insults her, in fact, he uses compliments (about her hands) to further increase her embarrassment.

The other key element of this situation is that Paul had an opportunity suddenly pop up (Lynne swinging her hand out), and he instantly seized it (no pun intended) and made the most of it. This is the difference between a guy who is a master at meeting girls, and the average guy who isn't. Guys like Paul and lots of the other guys that you've run into in this book make the most of opportunities. They don't think every situation to death, they act.

Obviously, in the above situation, if Paul had paused for even a second to think things over, the moment would have passed. For his move to work, he had to act right then, right when her arm was swinging. It's incredible how often these extremely brief opportunities for contact occur. If you're not prepared to take advantage of them, they will vanish as quickly as they appeared.

Meeting through a spontaneous event like this is much less stressful for the girl than just walking up to her cold. It's a natural meeting, and so everything that follows feels more natural as well.

Antidepressant

As I've mentioned before, when you first meet a girl, it's important to give the conversation a positive focus. The object is to present yourself as someone who is fun to be with and also stimulating. You can discuss her or your troubles some other time.

Preventing a conversation from straying into negative subjects isn't always that easy. Conversations are like branching roads. It's easy to mistakenly take a turn that leads to a depressing subject. Before you know it, the two of you are deep in some dark topic that you would have been better off avoiding.

This is not to say that you should avoid a tough subject at all costs. If the girl is having a hard time and really wants to discuss it, you can make a very positive impression by being a sympathetic listener. Still, more often than not, we get into these dismal subjects because we aren't thinking or because we are desperately trying to keep a conversation from dying. Try not to let that happen.

Stay sharp. When you feel the conversation slipping into the dumps, turn it around and head back out into the sunshine. You can be quite up front about this if necessary, saying, for example, "Hey, this is too much of a downer. We're here to have a good time, let's talk about something that's a little more upbeat." Most of the time, the girl will agree wholeheartedly.

In the following situation, Ray allows a conversation that started out well to go astray. Watch for the critical turning point where the conversation forks and heads into dismal territory. Ray is walking down the aisle at a busy dance spot when he happens on a girl who is laughing and dancing by herself right next to a table occupied by a couple of her friends.

Ray: You look like you're having a party all by yourself.

Sarah: Yes I am, big boy. (she holds up a playful fist) You got any complaints?

Ray: (laughs and raises his hands defensively) No way, I surrender.

Sarah: You better, 'cause I'm pretty tough.

Ray: I believe you. Maybe I should stay with you and talk. You seem to be having more fun than anyone else.

Sarah: I'm tryin'.

Ray: Can't do more than that. Why don't you and I go for a dance out on the floor?

Sarah: Thought you'd never ask. Let's go.

After dancing for about ten minutes, the two return to Sarah's table.

Ray:	You're a great dancer.
Sarah:	Thanks, you're not so bad yourself.
Ray:	How come I haven't seen you here before?
Sarah:	Darlin', I haven't been out dancing for two years.
Ray:	Get out of here! You're too good.
Sarah:	This is my first real night out in years, and I am enjoying it.
Ray:	So where have you been for two years?
Sarah:	It's a boring story.
Ray:	I promise I won't be bored.
Sarah:	Okay, you asked for it. I have been married to the most self-centered man in the entire universe, and the universe is a big place.
Ray:	You're married?
Sarah:	Not any more, not as of today. As of today, I am freeeee (waves her hand in the air).
Ray:	He didn't like to go out?
Sarah:	He didn't like to do anything, at least not with me, the bastard. He didn't have any problem doing things with his damn friends. And he didn't have any problem doing things with just about any other female he ran into—you know, all you men are worthless. I haven't run into one man that's worth...

Time to check out, Ray. Time to move on down the line. Your promising evening with this girl just evaporated. Sarah has gone from a girl who was determined to have a good time, to a girl who's angry and irritable. Worse, she's focused her anger about her ex-husband squarely on Ray. At this point, Ray might as well be her ex. He'll be lucky to get away without getting kicked in the crotch.

Think about this. Have you ever had a really great time while a certain song was being played in the background? After that, you always like that song because you associate it with pleasure. Hearing that song brings back those good feelings, and it makes you happy.

This theory about music also holds true with people. If a girl has a lot of fun and laughs after meeting you, that initial experience will create a strong favorable association—you equal good times in her mind, even in her subconscious mind.

The reverse is also true. If the two of you spend your first time together talking about depressing subjects, she may come to associate you with being unhappy, and that's not an association you want her to make. You always want her first impression of you to be one of positive feelings.

Understand that leaving a girl with a bad association doesn't necessarily mean that you argued with her, or had a hard time talking to her, or didn't get along with her. You may have had a long, interesting conversation. She may even have given you her phone number. But when you call to ask her out, something in the back of her head says no. That's a negative association. It leaves you asking yourself, "Why won't she go out with me? We had that deep, intimate conversation last night, and now she doesn't want to see me. What's the deal?"

The deal is that you had a painful or depressing conversation, and now when you contact her, she feels that pain all over again. Her conscious or subconscious mind has noted that you were present during an emotionally difficult event and has decided that you were the cause. To avoid repeating that distress, her emotional reaction is to stay away from you.

Slow Motion

Up to now, we've mostly discussed encounters set in places where there were lots of people around, such as busy bars, nightclubs, and parties. But what about the places that don't have the crowds, places that aren't as popular or aren't located in the prime nightlife areas?

Not so good you might think. Slow places obviously don't have as many women to select from. On the other hand, slow places don't have as much male competition. Nor do they have the same meat-market atmosphere in which girls can feel like targets. In a slow place, where everyone isn't trying to pick up everyone else, women are often calmer, friendlier, and less defensive.

In the next situation, Steve has been working late, and he decides to drop by a quiet local restaurant to get a bite to eat before going home. When he arrives at the restaurant, it's almost 9:30 and the one remaining waitress is cleaning up and getting ready to go home. Steve has been here before and knows the waitress. He asks her if he's too late to get some dinner. She says he's not and seats him a couple tables away from a blond (Carrie) who appears to be finishing up her own meal.

Waitress: Okay, Steve, what'll it be?

Steve: I guess I'll have this, the hot roast beef sandwich.

Waitress: (smiles) You know, you're not supposed to eat a big meal so late. Not good for you.

Steve: Ahh, I think you just want to go home.

Waitress: Steve, I'm hurt. I'm only thinking of your health.

Steve: (pointing to the blond) Did you warn her about eating a big meal too late?

Waitress: Well, I—

Steve: (to Carrie) Excuse me, did she warn you about the dangers of late night meals?

Carrie: She didn't have to. I only had a salad.

Steve: So!

Waitress: A salad is light, it's okay.

Steve: I think you ladies are ganging up on me.

Waitress: (laughs) Poor baby. (she leaves to put in Steve's order)

Steve: (to Carrie) So why are you eating your light meal so late?

Carrie: Work. We had to do inventory, and it takes forever. You?

Steve: Work too. I'm trying to finish up a presentation for Friday.

Carrie: Aren't we the hard working fools?

Steve: You aren't kidding. Say, since we're both such hard working pillars of the community, why don't you let me join you? I haven't talked to someone nice all day.

Carrie: I don't know, are you safe?
Steve: Yep, and I can get Alice (the waitress) to vouch for me.
Carrie: Well, all right. You seem okay.
Steve: (goes to her table and sits down) Thanks. I just want to make one rule.
Carrie: A rule, huh.
Steve: Right. And the rule is—we can talk about anything except work. I've had enough of work.
Carrie: Sounds good to me.
Steve: (Steve holds out his hand and they shake) My name is Steve.
Carrie: Carrie.
Steve: Nice name, I like it.
Carrie: Thanks.

Steve and Carrie talk for thirty minutes and then Carrie indicates she has to leave.

Carrie: I'm having a great time, but I really do have to get home.
Steve: Well, I don't see a ring, so I suppose you aren't married. Why don't we get together again?
Carrie: You're right, I'm not married.
Steve: (smiles) Not attached in any way, shape, or form?
Carrie: Not in any way, shape, or form.
Steve: This is my big chance to ask for your phone number then.
Carrie: (to the waitress) Alice, should I give this

	gentleman my phone number?
Waitress:	He's got bad eating habits, but he's normal enough.
Carrie:	Well, okay then. I usually don't do this, but I will this time.
Waitress:	(to Steve) You've had quite a night, haven't you?
Steve:	Better than I ever hoped.

Steve might never have done so well at the hottest bar in town. Here are some other advantages of meeting a woman in a slow, unexciting place.

The noise level in a busy bar or dance club can make intimate conversation almost impossible. Unless you look like a movie star, one of your biggest assets when you meet a girl is conversation. But it's hard to have a real talk when you have to scream at the top of your voice to be heard over the music and the noise created by a large crowd.

Another advantage in the above situation is that Steve was able to use his friendship with the waitress, Alice, to pave the way for him. Obviously, girls are often apprehensive when they meet a male they don't know. They can't be sure that a stranger is a safe person to let into their life. Many a guy has been turned down not because the girl found him unattractive, but because she just didn't want to take the risk of giving her phone number or address to a stranger.

Carrie was probably on the fence about giving Steve her number. It was Steve's good relationship with Alice, and Alice's confirmation that he could be trusted, that tipped

Carrie his way. In a jam-packed bar, it is unlikely that these events could have played out similarly. In the popular nightlife spots, women are often more edgy and distrustful while men seem more flaky and menacing. The moral of this story—don't write off a place just because it's not the hottest hangout in town.

Battle of the Sexes

Whenever a guy attempts to meet and charm a woman, it can be a high-pressure event for all parties, men and women alike. Sometimes all that intensity causes a situation to erupt into confrontation or bad feelings.

Rejection, or even the perception of being rejected, is hard to take, and it's not uncommon for guys who have been told no to retaliate with insults or spiteful wisecracks. Women too can find the whole process of being approached by strange men stressful, and they may also react with sharp comments or impatient behavior.

None of this should be surprising. Lots of things that are centrally important to people are being put at risk here. Consider this partial list of potentially trouble-making factors that can come into play any time a man puts the make on a woman—ego, dignity, status, failure, pride, fear, resentment, jealousy, self-esteem, shame, lust, anger, embarrassment, privacy, suspicion, discouragement, indignation, exasperation, humiliation, guilt, confusion, cynicism, misunderstanding, and, last but not least, alcohol. When you consider all these hazards, it's a marvel that men and women can ever tiptoe through this emotional minefield without triggering an explosion.

Here's a situation in which everyone involved seems to plant a foot squarely on a hidden mine. Standing at the bar of a downtown nightclub, Daren and Shaun have been watching three attractive girls for half an hour. Finally, after much hesitation and numerous delaying tactics, their fear that someone else will grab the girls seems to overpower their fear of rejection. Summoning their courage, they each toss down one more margarita and then stride across the room toward the unsuspecting girls. The three girls are engrossed in their own conversation, laughing, and more than a little drunk.

Daren: Excuse me. Hi, how are you girls doing tonight?

The girls, who hadn't seen the guys coming, break off their happy discussion and turn toward the guys.

Ashley: Did you say something?
Daren: Uh, yeah…what's going on?
Ashley: What's going on? We're having some drinks and talking, that's what's going on.
Lori: Can we help you?
Shaun: Well, we just thought you might like some company.
Lori: Do we look lonely?
Kay: I don't think we're lonely. I know I'm not.
Ashley: (to Daren) Sounds like you're the ones who need some company.

Daren:	Hey, we didn't mean to interrupt you, sorry.
Lori:	Well good, I'm glad we got that settled. See ya.
Kay:	Yeah, see ya.
Shaun:	Look, you don't have to be so snippy about it. We said we were sorry if we interrupted.
Kay:	Uh-huh, but you're still here, dudes. We were kind of hoping to be seeing your backs by now.
Daren:	Hey, you know something, what is wrong with you chicks? You fuckin' act like you all think you're Pamela Anderson or something. Believe me, you're not as hot as you think.
Ashley:	Listen, who walked over to whose table here, anyway?
Shaun:	What's the big deal? You came here to meet guys didn't you?
Ashley:	Who says we came here to meet guys?
Daren:	(gives Shaun a knowing look) Oh, I get it.
Kay:	Oh, give me a break, you don't get shit!
Ashley:	Yeah, take a hike.
Daren:	No problem, we're out of here. You girls just cuddle up together again.
Lori:	Screw you.
Ashley:	Yeah, who lets guys like you in here, anyway?
Shaun:	(with a big, exaggerated wave) Bye, bye, ladies, have a good time together.
Daren:	Hey, Shaun, let's go talk to those girls over there. They look like they're here to meet men.
Ashley:	Yes, please, go give those girls the benefit of your fabulous personalities.
Shaun:	Bitches.

Whew, that went well. All right, so what happened here? Daren and Shaun probably aren't bad guys, but they did unintentionally set themselves up for trouble with these girls. Their first error was to intrude so crudely on the girls' little party. They didn't try to find a smooth or natural way to insert themselves, they just made a forced entry. The girls, who were involved in an enjoyable conversation, were understandably miffed by this uninvited and unexpected disruption of their chatty talk.

So, the meeting of these guys and girls was off to a bad start, but the guys could still have saved the day if they had followed through with something entertaining or stimulating, something that would convince the girls that the interruption was worthwhile. Unfortunately, they did not. Daren's less than enticing opener, "Uh, yeah…what's going on?" will hardly make the girls feel they had been disturbed for good reason. The guys are basically asking the girls to trade a delightful conversation among themselves for a boring conversation with them. What a deal! No wonder the girls' annoyance quickly shows.

Still, the girls are pretty hard on Daren and Shaun, probably because their manners have been liberally diluted by alcohol. It isn't long before the guys are losing face big time and feel like they have to fight back. Once they do, the battle is on.

Frankly, although few guys would have had the self-control to ignore some of these girls' rude comments, from a purely practical standpoint, that is what they should have done. Once they saw that the girls perceived them as party crashers, Daren and Shaun should have apologized sincerely and beat a hasty retreat, avoiding any reaction to the girls' remarks. If they had, who knows, it's possible that the girls might have felt so guilty that they would have given the guys a second chance later on, or on another occasion. But after their big war, the guys have no chance at all, and these girls may even bad-mouth them to other girls in the nightclub, further reducing Daren and Shaun's opportunities.

Figure This One Out

Lurking in the following episode is probably one of the most important lessons of this book. I won't point it out right now. See if you can discover what it is. The only hint that I'll give you is this—becoming highly skilled in meeting girls requires a certain mind-set or outlook on life. Once you're aware of what this mind-set is, you'll probably realize that most of the guys you know who are good at meeting women have it.

John has just pulled up to the gas pumps at a service station. On the other side of the pumps, a somewhat overweight, average-looking girl has just started to fill up her own car, a small Honda. John gives her the once over and knows that she isn't really his type, at least as far as looks are concerned.

John: (smiles) How often do you have to fill up that Honda. Once every two months?

Cheryl: (smiles back) I wish. It is pretty good on gas, but it's not that good.

John: (points to his own car) It's gotta be better than my car. There are entire oil fields in Saudi

|||||||||||||||||||||||||||||||

Arabia that are totally dedicated to producing gas just for my car.

Cheryl: (laughs) So that's why gas is so expensive. Your car is using up all the supply.

John: Probably. If my car were junked today, the price of gas would probably drop 15 cents.

Cheryl: I was considering getting a car like yours a while back. But I didn't

John: Best decision you ever made. I haven't been able to afford to eat anything but macaroni and cheese since I got this thing.

Cheryl: You look pretty fit for a guy on a straight macaroni and cheese diet.

John: I also use up a lot of energy pushing the car when it breaks down.

Cheryl: Oh, it breaks down too. It really does sound like a lot of fun to own.

John: You have no idea.

Cheryl: (putting the gas nozzle back in the pump) Well, it's been nice talking to you.

John: Nice talking to you. Take good care of that Honda.

Cheryl: I will. Bye.

John: See ya.

So what's the big lesson here? All John did was talk. He made no effort to get the girl's phone number or to see her again. As I said before, she really wasn't his type. I'll give you another hint.

Suppose you decided that more than anything in the

world you wanted to be a great baseball player. You love everything about the game—the crack of the bat when it makes solid ball contact, the roar of the crowd, the thrill of victory, the agony of defeat, and so on. More than anything, you want to be a hot player, a player who is in demand. There is only one problem—you refuse to participate in baseball practice. The only time you will play is during a real, official, bet-it-all game.

Would that make sense? Clearly not. How could you ever develop your skills if you refused to practice? Could you reach your potential by limiting your play to official games only? It's unlikely that you could. Baseball, like most skills, requires regular and frequent practice. That practice is designed to hone your skills and build your confidence so that you are ready when the big game finally comes. Without this training, the competition cleans your clock.

By now I'm sure you get the point. It doesn't have to be Saturday night for you to say hello to a girl you don't know, and a girl shouldn't have to be totally beautiful before you will open a conversation with her.

Just as with accurately throwing a baseball, skillfully opening and maintaining a conversation with a girl is in large part a learned skill. The more practice you get, the better you'll be, and in turn, the less threatening it will seem. If you only make the effort to talk to a girl when she's BEAUTIFUL or when she's exactly YOUR TYPE, your chance of charming her with your confidence and style won't be as high as it would have been if you made it a habit to talk to female strangers all the time. So remember, practice makes perfect.

And what is the mind-set that I referred to at the beginning of this chapter, the mind-set that girl-getting guys often seem to have? Guys who are really good with women really like women—*all* women, not just the totally hot, totally beautiful ones. They thoroughly enjoy talking to them and being with them. As a result, they are more likely to strike up conversations and make contact in general. And each time they approach and interact with the opposite sex, they get better at it.

No Go

We have now come to our final conversation. There's not much need for an explanation of this one. This is a situation that will be quite familiar to almost every guy who has ever approached a girl. The setting is a crowded local bar. Matt watches as some people brush past a girl standing near him, almost causing her to spill her drink.

Matt: Pretty crazy in here tonight, isn't it?
Vicki: What do you mean?
Matt: Crowded. No room to move.
Vicki: Uh-huh.
Matt: Believe it or not, it'll get worse later.
Vicki: (staring off into the crowd) What?
Matt: I said it'll get more crowded later.
Vicki: Oh.
Matt: Hold on tight to your drink.
Vicki: Why?
Matt: Because it's so—never mind. You having a good time tonight?
Vicki: Uh-huh.
Matt: They have a band coming on in about twenty

	minutes, and they're not bad. I've heard them before.
Vicki:	That's good.
Matt:	I'm Matt. What's your name?
Vicki:	Why do you need to know that?
Matt:	Uh, I guess I don't need to know it. I just thought it would help.
Vicki:	Help what?
Matt:	The conversation. If I can use your name, you'll know for sure that I'm talking to you and not someone else.
Vicki:	You're a funny guy.
Matt:	Thank you. So what is your name?
Vicki:	Look, I'm just waiting for a friend. I don't need any company, okay?
Matt:	No problem.
Vicki:	(turns her back and faces the bar)
Matt:	Nice meeting you.

Has this ever happened to you? If it hasn't, you are a very lucky guy. You're so lucky, in fact, that you should be out buying lottery tickets right now; you're sure to win. For the rest of us though, rejection or complete disinterest from a girl is not an unknown experience.

A good survival tip is not to read too much into a bad experience like the one Matt just suffered through. It's easy for a guy who has been rejected to assume that it was due to his looks, personality, and so on. Don't be hard on yourself. It only makes it tougher to find the courage to approach the next girl.

The fact is that Matt has no idea why Vicki didn't take an

interest in him. Maybe she's angry because she caught her boyfriend sleeping around earlier that day, maybe she was fired from her job, maybe she's waiting for a jealous boyfriend, or maybe someone just backed into her car in the bar's parking lot.

There are always lots of reasons for a girl to seem disinterested, and the vast majority of them have nothing to do with you personally. The important lesson here is to refuse to allow a bad experience with one girl to keep you from approaching the next girl. Why? Because that next girl may very well be the one that thinks you're wonderful at first sight.

Conclusion

That's all folks. The previous pages have given you a lot to think about. Clearly, every first meeting between a guy and a girl is unique. These situations move and change directions too quickly for you to be able to solve the problem of uncertainty by memorizing what you are going to say in advance or by trying the same approach with every girl you meet. You have to be flexible. You have to be able to tell which way the wind is blowing and then go with it. That's the most important skill you can have, and there's only one way to develop that skill—you have to talk to lots of different girls in lots of different environments.

After you've met a girl, whether things went well or badly, ask yourself how you could have done better. Calmly and rationally analyze your performance. Don't beat yourself up if it didn't work out well. If she didn't go for you, don't assume that it was because you have some fatal and permanent flaw in your appearance or sex appeal. The point of this analysis is to improve your skills with women, not to thrash your self-confidence within an inch of its life. Don't ever ask "What's wrong with *me*?" Focus strictly on improvement. Asking "How can I do better the next time?"

will direct you along a more productive path.

When we approach a girl who doesn't respond well, most of us automatically blame something basic and unchangeable in ourselves. The result is that we are even more insecure and clumsy the next time we approach a female. To help break this vicious cycle, keep the following three points in mind.

- There are thousands of reasons for a girl to be unresponsive, and most of them have nothing to do with you personally (for instance, she may be worried that the people she is with will tell her boyfriend if she talks too much with any one guy).
- Girls rarely reject a guy strictly on the basis of looks. I don't mean that they don't care about looks, but it is not as important to a girl as it is to a guy. Any guy who projects strength, confidence, and a sense of humor can overcome the looks barrier.
- Failure is most often related to a guy's approach. The good news here is that you can change and improve your approach if you work at it. Girls are far more likely to reject a guy because he is nervous, awkward, boring, or overly assertive than because of his appearance. Practice can eliminate any problem related to one's approach.

One other thought—girls are generally more intrigued by guys they can't quite capture. As long as she knows you have the power to walk away from her, you have the upper hand. If you are too nice, too desperate, too obviously needy, she will sense it, and it definitely won't turn her on.

In a misguided effort to make girls like them, many guys try way too hard to exhibit an exaggerated niceness. Don't! Maintain some tension, keep her a little off balance and a little uncomfortable. I'm not telling you to be hard to live with, standoffish, argumentative, impolite, or insulting, but I am telling you to maintain some element of reserve in your demeanor.

For example, let girls know you think they're sexy, but don't let them think you'd sell your soul to be with them. Guys who are successful with girls often use compliments liberally, but the look in their eye and the tone of their voice tells the girl she could still lose him. Girls respect a guy who maintains his self-respect.

If you put yourself out there, refusing to be intimidated by rejection, talking to more and more girls, you will develop a very high level of skill and style. None of this can be learned by solitary contemplation or by hanging out with your buddies. It can only be learned by putting yourself in front of a stranger of the opposite sex and interacting with her. If you do this, and keep doing this, you will find that the rejections become increasingly rare and the good times increasingly frequent.